# Poems of Power, Purpose and Praise

I0149461

### Sherry A. Johnson

**Published
By**

PMJ Productions
P.O. Box 833
Prairie View, Texas 77446
(832) 377-1352
PSOJ_23@yahoo.com

Printed in the United States of America

ISBN: (13) 978-0-9822227-9-9

ISBN: (10) 0-9822227-9-3

# Acknowledgement

This project would not have been realized without the love and support of the following influences in my life:

- Our Heavenly Father, who entrust me with the gift of writing and the inspiration to compile these poems.
- My husband, Dr. Paul Johnson, whose love, encouragement, and artistic ability complement my life.
- Bishop Hero Blair, and the congregation of Faith Cathedral Deliverance Center (104) , for providing a solid foundation for my faith to grow and a place I can always call home.
- Pastor Allan Abney, who provides food for my soul and revelation on how to give myself to God.
- Our sons, Paul Jr., Sherdayne and Jaydon whose unconditional love motivates me when I am down.
- My mother Hermine Jackson whose life experiences is a source of inspiration.
- My friends, Sharon, Cochetta and Lois who believe in me and my God-given assignment.

# Table of Contents

# Introduction

I do not know where you are, what you do on a daily basis, or the time of day it is as you take time out of your schedule to read these words. Although we may or may not have met, I would like to remind you that you are a special and unique individual who was **Created for Success**! Amidst life's struggles and obstacles however, you may have questioned your purpose, felt **Unworthy,** or may have even declared its not easy **Being Me**. You may have pondered issues from your past, and **On Bended Knees**, cried out **Forgive Me Lord,** or **Remind Me Lord,** as your soul longed for **Perfect Peace** and **Breakthrough**. There is **No Expiration Date** on **Needing God**! **God's Compassion**, His mercy and **Grace** abound towards you, the apple of His eyes – His **Chosen** One. Regardless of how you may have felt in the past, or how you may feel presently, remember in whose image you were created. *God said, Let Us [Father, Son and Holy Ghost] make mankind in Our Image, after Our likeness, and let them have complete authority over the fish of the sea, the birds of the air, the [tame] beasts, and over all of the earth, and over everything that creeps upon the earth. (Genesis 1:26).*

**Stop and Reflect** on the fact that you are made in **God's Image and Likeness!** Because you are made in the image and likeness of the Omniscient and Omnipotent **God Almighty,** you are equipped with the knowledge, wisdom and understanding needed for you to dominate the earth. **Don't Give In** to the lies of the devil. You have been **Set Free,** from all sins – past, present and future. *"There is therefore now, no condemnation to them which are in Christ Jesus, who walks not after the flesh, but after the Spirit." (Romans 8:1)* **Through the Blood** of Jesus Christ, you have been reconciled unto God, and are now free to tap into the **Truth** of who you are **Without Condemnation**!

Society, situations and circumstances may attempt to bombard you with negativity, based on: your ethnicity; your physical appearance; your socio-economic status; your gender; your age; your level of education and the list continues. None of those things matter when you are in Christ, so give yourself permission to **Step Away From Negativity** and from people and situations that will cause you doubts. In the quilted tapestry of humanity, we are woven together as one in Christ; but it is our differences that make  it possible for us to add meaning and value to each others' lives.  Let not society, family, friends, acquaintances, past, present or future experiences prevent you from seeing the true you. You are a **Child of Almighty God**, **Chosen**, and **Anointed**.  You are **Called by God** and **Empowered for Greatness,** before you were even born. *Before I formed you in the womb I knew [and] approved of you [as My chosen instrument], and before you were born I separated and set you apart, consecrating you; [and] appointed you as a prophet to the nations. (Jeremiah 1:5)*

Whether you are walking in God's ordained plan for your life and are assured that His purpose for you is being manifested; or you are on the periphery of doubt, or on a quest to determine the purpose for which the **Creator** has made you; rest assured that your best days are yet to come! *I am convinced and sure of this very thing; that He who began a good work in you will continue until the day of Jesus Christ [right up to the time of His return], developing [that good work] and perfecting and bringing it to full completion in you. (Philippians 1:6)*

# POWER

*Yours, O Lord, is the greatest and the power and the glory and the victory and the majesty for all that is in the heavens and in the earth is yours. Yours is the kingdom, O Lord, and You are exalted as head above all.*
**(1 Chronicles 29: 11)**

*Be exalted, O Lord, in your strength! We will sing and praise Your power.*
**(Psalms 21:13)**

*It is He who made the earth by His power, who established the world by His wisdom, and by His understanding stretched out the heavens.*
**(Jeremiah 10: 12)**

*But you will receive power when the Holy Spirit has com upon you, and you will be my witnesses in Jerusalem and in all Judea and Samaria, and to the end of the earth.*
**(Acts 1:8)**

# A Lady After God's Own Heart!

Father, at the end of my days
After I've done my work on earth,
May I be remembered by family and friends,
As "A lady after God's own heart."

I commit this day to service
Being Your hands, eyes and feet.
I pledge to touch the lives of people,
Regardless of how or where we meet.

Lord, I invite Your presence daily,
To guide and direct my ways.
I dedicate my life to honor You,
And to being Your instrument of praise.

Lord, I have come to the realization
I'm a testimony of Your Favor personified,
So I will live my life to Your glory,
And faithfully serve You for the rest of my life.

*(Psalms 132: 1-4)*

# Anoint Me Oh Lord

Anoint me Oh Lord,
To be a messenger for You.
Touch my heart…
Touch my mind…
Touch my lips…
Before You are through.

Anoint me Oh Lord,
To be on fire for You.
Guide my thoughts…
Guide my path…
Guide my steps…
As I work for You.

Anoint me Oh Lord,
To be a vessel of honor for You.
Preserve my joy…
Preserve my faith…
Preserve my worship…
As I testify about You

# Being Me

It's not easy being all I can be.
I struggle daily with the sinful me.
Temptations weighing me down,
As sin crouch at my heart's door.

In this imperfect being,
Plagued with pain and suffering.
Lifelong wounds pound within my heart,
Reminding me of mistakes I made.

It's not easy being all I can be.
I struggle daily with the sinful me.
Temptations weighing me down,
As sin crouch at my heart's door.

So Lord, I cast it all to You,
All my fears and worries too.
I'll keep Your Words within my heart,
And my eyes I'll fix on You.

It's not easy being all I can be.
I struggle daily with the sinful me.
Temptations weighing me down,
As sin crouch at my heart's door.

*(Romans 7: 15 – 24)*

## Child of Almighty God

Be convinced in who you are,
Child of Almighty God!
Compromise not your standard
Nor your character.
When temptation or adversity tries to set in.
Remember that the God of the Creation,
He abides within.

Stand up!
Be proud of who you are,
You are the Child of Almighty God!

Your father is the God of the Universe,
Favor and blessing is upon your life.
It is impossible for you to fail,
Cause you've been called to fulfill His will.

## Dare to Dream.

Like the eagle among birds,
So am I among men.
I can see above and beyond my eyes limitations,
Cause I operate based on what I create
On the canvas of my imagination.

I have been blessed with knowledge
And understanding of who I am.
So I walk by faith, and not by sight,
As I journey throughout this land.

God created me a leader with a vision,
So I focus not on private ambition,
But commit to achieving synergy,
In every facet of life, in every situation.

I will be more than a tombstone
Cause I have a vision to impart.
My dreams will impact this nation,
And generations not yet alive.

*(Proverbs 29:18; Genesis 1:26)*

# Don't Give In!

The devil comes across my path,
In various disguises,
Promising remedies for problems I'm facing.
He shows me a way out,
If I'll just listen,
To the sound of his voice,
And the lies he's preaching.
I won't  give in!


The devil promises fame, power and glory,
Things he cannot fulfill,
Because he doesn't own it.
He tries to get me to bow down to him,
Discouraged, disgruntled, distracted within.

He tries to prevent me from embracing The Truth-
Jesus is The Answer
For whatever I'm facing.
I will continue through Christ to resist his lies
I won't give in to him.

*(Psalms 118:6; 1John 3:19 – 22; 1 John 5:4-8)*

# Empowered for Greatness

In all that you do,
Do it unto the Lord wholeheartedly.
God can see your impact,
Even when it is not clear to you.

In this world you can make a difference,
Because God resides in you.
He will empower and direct you,
In everything you do.

Trust the Lord with your talents and skills,
They're not too small to be used.
When you give selflessly unto the Lord,
He will use you supernaturally.

# Faithful Sowers

There's an initiating source,
That begins the process
Of seedtime and harvest
For fruits to multiply and manifest.

God provides the seeds,
And God calls the sower.
The quality of the seed,
Is not determine by quantity
But the quality of that which is sown.

God is looking for faithful sowers,
Who will plant the seeds He gives.
While the earth remains, this fact remains true,
There'll be seedtime and harvest,
For as long as we live.

# Enter

Enter The Truth.
Follow the voice of Jesus.
He's calling you forward,
So your blessings you will behold,
As you receive the truth and knowledge of God's Word.


Your spirit, soul and body,
Belongs to Almighty God,
Get into deeper depths,
Climb higher heights,
Devour the word of God,
And receive revelation truth.


Feed your soul the truth of God,
A healthy soul dictates to your emotions what to feel,
It advises your mind what to think,
And  instructs your will what to do.
Enter into the word of God and receive revelation truth.

Stay no longer on the shores of life,
Step out in faith into the deep.
Enter into the word,
Enter the presence of God,
Enter and receive revelation truth.

*(Mark 8: 36; Philippians 3:14;*
*1Thessalonians 5: 23- 24;*
*Psalms 42: 4- 8;  Psalms 26:7)*

## Faith-driven

Lord, I stand in faith,
Believing for an increased measure.
There's an earnest desire inside of me,
That has awakened an unquenchable longing
For more and more of Thee.

Lord, I meditate upon Your Word,
And secure it in my heart.
My level of sight is based upon my faith,
And the things I hope for in Thee.

Lord, I live by my conviction
That all things are possible for You.
My life is not regulated by my five senses,
But by what Your Word declares.

## Force of Faith

Everything starts with an idea,
A thought conceived in the mind.
The thought then comes to life,
When one acts in accordance to faith.

The just shall live by faith,
Not based upon what we see.
God's thoughts are not our thoughts,
And at times don't make sense naturally.

Rely not on human rationale
To get your needs met.
If you will simply believe and trust God,
Then all things are possible.

Allow your natural mind to be convinced.
About that which God has spoken.
God is declaring a new reality,
That exists for those who'll walk by faith and trust Him.

*Philippians 4:19; Acts 16:25; 1 Timothy 6:12; 1 Peter 2:24; 1 Samuel*
*21: 1-15; Ezekiel 46:9 –11; Isaiah 8:18*

## Forgive Yourself

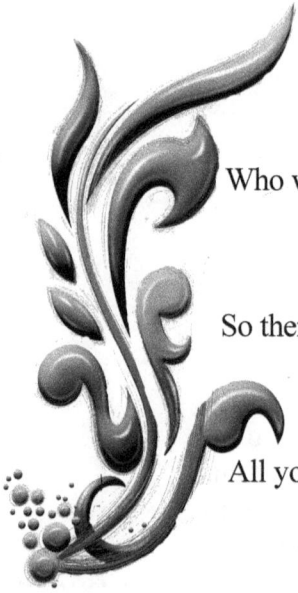

I am forgiven!
All my sins and iniquities are forgotten!
I refuse to listen to the lies of the accuser,
Who wants to condemn me, based upon past mistakes.

The loving and kind God that I serve,
Chose to forgive and forget my sins.
So there's no need to dwell upon the wrongs I've done,
All I need to do is to forgive myself.

My friend, you are forgiven!
All your sins and iniquities, past, present and future…
Are all forgotten!

Choose this day to refuse to listen,
To the lies of the accuser,
Who wants to torment you,
And condemns you,
Based upon past mistakes.

All our sins and iniquities are forgiven and forgotten,
The moment we asked Jesus to come in.

## Greatness

Lord, I know You have greater things…
Greater things for me to do.
Your word promises that You'll see me through the very
end
If I trust and obey You.

Confidently, I confront conflicts created by doubts
Not by myself, but with Your Holy Spirit
Who empowers me from within.

Resting assured upon Your Word,
I face difficulties with the boldness of a lion,
Through the righteousness of Jesus Christ,
And His promises to man.

# Go Before Me Lord

Go before me Lord,
And lead me where I should follow.
You've lead the children of Israel,
Out of Egypt's fury, despair and slavery,
So surely, if I trust You, You will lead me too.

I do not need plagues, signs or wonders,
Just a clear word from You.
I will go through my wilderness experience,
Cause somewhere You've prepared a place,
Where my blessings will flow.

In everything I do,
Lead me in the path of righteousness.
Leave no room for error or misinterpretation,
In the strategic maneuvering of my life's success.

So I won't lose momentum along the journey,
But rather depend upon You.
Build my trust. Build my faith. Build my confidence.
Be my compass. Be my cloud. Be my  pillar of fire.

***The Book of  Exodus***

# Help Me to Listen

Lord, speak to me today,
And help me to listen.
Let me hear Your voice,
And recognize You speaking.

Touch my heart,
And awaken my faith,
Intensify my desire to follow You,
And the love and awe I have for You.

Lord, I throw myself at Your feet,
Waiting to hear from You.
Speak to me today,
And help me to listen.

*(Luke 17)*

# Holding On

Father, Your word declares,
You'll never give us more than we can bear,
So, I'll wait upon You,
And be of good cheer.

*(2 Corinthians 12:8)*

Your Holy Spirit is my helper,
Father, I know I'm never alone.
I'll hold fast and without wavering,
To the promises yet to come.

*(Philippians 4:7; Psalm 2:1)*

I am choosing to live by faith,
Though temptations come my way,
I will diligently seek You Father,
Help me to trust, obey and pray.

*(1 John 1:9; 2 Corinthians 3:17; James 2:17)*

# I am More

I am more than what you see,
When you take a moment,
To glance towards me.

I am more than what you perceive,
Cause through Christ Jesus,
I've been set free.

I am more than what society dictates,
Cause there's no boundary set,
Within which I must operate.

I am more than what you can process,
Cause God's grace and favor,
Guarantees my success.

I am more than what you believe,
Cause commanded blessings,
Are constantly flowing towards me.

# I Can Let Go!

I can let go Lord, and simply trust You.
I can let go Lord, and put my faith in You.
I can let go Lord, and rest assured in You.
I can let go, because You'll never let go of me.

I can let go, because You'll never let go of me.
I can let go, because You'll never let go of me.

I can let go Lord, and simply love You.
I can let go Lord, and praise and honor You.
I can let go Lord, and give my heart to You.
I can let go, because You'll never let go of me.

You'll never let go, You'll never let go,
You'll never let go of me. (Repeat)
I can let go, because You'll never let go of me.

## I'm Excited Lord

I'm excited Lord,
About what You're doing in me.
I'm excited Lord,
Because from sin You've set me.
I'm excited Lord, because of You.
I'm excited Lord, because of You.

I'm excited Lord,
Because You've renewed my heart and mind.
I'm excited Lord,
Because from me you'll never depart.
I'm excited Lord, because of You.
I'm excited Lord, because of You.

I'll sing You praises Lord,
Every day from the moment I rise.
I'll sing You praises Lord,
Till the moment I close my eyes.
I'm excited Lord, because of you.
I'm excited Lord, because of You.

## I Will Trust You

Lord, I invite You in,
To be the Master of my life.
Even in the small things I do,
I will trust You.

I will listen to Your voice,
Even if doubts set in.
I will cry out and wait upon you because…
I will trust You.

I will seek Your face,
When life gets complicated.
When all seem shattered and in dismay,
Lord, I will trust You.

# Increase My Sensitivity

No matter what state I am in,
Lord, You're still trying to get to me.
Your voice is a familiar sound,
Very distinct and clear telling me where to turn.

Increase my sensitivity to your voice Lord,
So I may grow in statue and might.
My heart is now receptive to Your word,
With my whole heart I now search for You
Knowing You will be found.

Let me see with the eyes of my heart,
And hear through my heart's ear.
My soul seeks to respond to You,
So my heart can fulfill its origin function.

*(John 17:21; Isaiah 55:8; Genesis 3:8-10; Malachi 3:6)*

# Keep Me Lord

May I see a glimpse of Your glory,
And see You in Your power.
Give me a wakeup call,
And keep me from potential fury.

May I not get so far off course
Where I forget Your eternal power.
May I not get caught up in pressures and strife
To the point where I forget that You are life.

Lord, I am reminded that You are calm,
But have the power to bring thunder and storm.
Help me to keep my attention where it needs to be
So that from destruction, I will be free.

Lord, when I get distracted
Help me to stop and reflect.
May I consider the great things You've done,
With a heart that's softened
And filled with gratitude and love.

*(1 Samuel 12)*

## Lord, I Come

Lord, I come to You this day,
With my knees bent,
With my voice lifted,
And my heart filled with thanksgiving
To praise and worship You.

Lord, I come to You,
With my spirit rekindled,
With only one desire
To love and honor you.

Lord, I come to you,
With music in my being,
With a song on my lips,
To dance before You, The King of Kings.

## My Purpose

Day in, day out I am here.
What is the real purpose I am here?
It must be beyond self!
It must be beyond worldly achievement,
And peer recognition!
What is my purpose?

I was created to glorify God.
My sole purpose is to live for the Almighty.
I was created to be set apart.
I was born to be an example.
I was called to love and serve others.
Day in, day out I am here.
I am here to glorify God.

## No Expiration Date

Wow! There's no expiration date
On the gift of eternal life.
Once I accept that gift,
In my heart, Jesus will live!

Wow! There's no expiration date,
On the path to forgiveness,
It does not matter where or when I was born,
Jesus can still be mine.

Wow! There's no expiration date,
On the love Jesus has for me,
He proclaims blessing and favor on my life,
Before I was born until eternity.

# Path to Self-discovery

The path to self discovery,
To understanding who you are,
May be plagued with numerous obstacles,
But it is a journey worth taking.

Once you discover the reason you were created,
And start living out your full potential,
You will experience joy and fulfillment,
And peace that defies all understanding.

Any type of healing needed,
It can be found in God.
He welcomes your vulnerabilities,
And promises restoration in every aspect of life.

Linger not, nor be emotionally withdrawn.
Spend time with The Almighty.
Be not ashamed to expose yourself,
As you journey along the path to self-discovery.

*(Philippians 4:7; Psalms 107:20)*

# Peace

Direct my heart Oh Lord,
Into your unwavering love.
Let my mind be consumed with You,
As You draw me closer to thee.

Console my heart Oh Lord,
As I rest in Your endless peace.
Let me not be anxious for anything,
But instead, pray without ceasing.

Guard my heart Oh Lord,
As I put my trust in You.
Let my thoughts be true and pure,
In everything I say and do.

# Power of Thinking

A negative image is like a parasite,
Attacking slowly, but surely.
Eating away at your confidence,
Latching on, penetrating,
Pulling you towards indulgence.

A positive image is like a catalyst,
Empowering you to believe the impossible.
It creates vision for the unchartered territories,
Taking you on mental exploits and unique voyages.

A positive image guide you to the right place,
Where you will connect with the god-like you.
It beckons you to  seek more of God
In whose image and likeness you were created.

*(Romans 4; Job 36:5)*

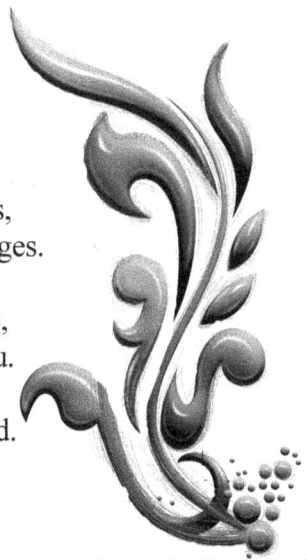

# Special to God

God is not a respecter of persons.
He has no favorites among men.
Each person is special to Him,
And everyone's welcomed in His sight.

God desires to bless you.
Bless you above all nations.
He wants to purposefully place you,
In the area where your blessing will flow.

Don't doubt your contribution,
And that which you have to offer.
You have what it takes to make a difference,
Therefore, let not the devil rob your confidence.

Make the call of God your priority,
And establish where you are suppose to be.
Make the call the foundation of your life,
And your efforts will never end in futility.

*(Joshua 1: 1-8; Isaiah 51; Job 8:7; 2 Peter1:10)*

# Standing Firm

Lord, I am in the valley of life…
Waiting on You.
My enemies are circling around.
In the middle of this battle
I sometimes forget what to do.

Circled by a series of crisis,
I'm sometimes nervous.
Doubt, dismay and discouragement...
are hovering about.
Fear threatens to cripple me.
So unto you, Almighty God,
I lift my voice and shout!

I carry a lot of baggage,
My shoulder gets weary.
So Father, I am standing firm on your promises
That you'll never leave nor forsake me.

Jehovah, I know you will deliver me.
Amidst the struggles of life
I put my trust in thee.
You are the True and Living God,
The rock on which I stand.
My hope is fixed upon you,
As I journey throughout this land.

*(Galatians 6:9; Isaiah 40:31; Proverbs 3:6)*

# Stepping Out By Faith

LORD, I am stepping out today.
I am stepping out , from a life of mediocrity.
I am stepping out, from desires crippled with fear.
I am stepping out, from anxiety and worrying.
I am stepping out, by faith.

LORD, I am stepping out today.
I am stepping out, from procrastination.
I am stepping out, from confusion and condemnation,
I am stepping out as You beckon me to come.
I am stepping out, by faith.

LORD, I am stepping out today.
I am  stepping out, from depression and dejection.
I am stepping out, from stereotype and rejection.
I am stepping out to gain empowerment,
I am stepping out, by faith.

LORD, I am stepping out today.
I am stepping out, to claim my destiny.
I am stepping out, to reach my testimony.
I am stepping out, to walk beside you.
I am stepping out, by faith.

# Vision. You Have It!

Vision is a call from God Almighty.
It's a seed He plants in your heart.
It allows you to see where others are blind,
Because you have the word of God,
Breaking barriers conceived in the mind.

God will never call you
And leave you empty-handed.
He knows the demands your vision will require,
And has already spoken to men,
To supply your heart's desire.

God has called you,
To make an impact in this generation.
The advancement of humanity is in your hands,
Let not experience, feelings, labels or geography close your mind,
But rather feed your vision with faith-filled meditation.

*Proverbs 29:18; Genesis 1:26; Exodus 36:1-2; Mark 3:13;*
*Matthew 3:1; Isaiah 40:3; John 5:30*

# Walking with God

Lord, walking with You
Has not always been easy.
It's a journey sometimes crippled
With ignorance and pride,
Requiring at times much needed sacrifice.


Lord, sometimes I forget
And walk away from You.
I get stuck and walk backwards
Cause my eyes drifted from You.
Lord, sometimes I stumble,
As I walk towards You.
But I get up with determination
Knowing You'll carry me through.


Lord, my desire is to walk by faith,
With my eyes fixed upon You.
Regardless of where I am,
I know You are there too.
Lord confidently I walk forward,
In my desire to worship You.
I know You hold my hand,
So I can let go of self and simply trust You.

# PURPOSE

*I know that you can do all things,*
*and that no purpose of yours can be thwarted.*
***(Job 42:2)***

*Many are the plans in the mind of a man,*
*but it is the purpose of the Lord that will stand.*
***(Proverbs 19:21)***

*The Lord has done what He purposed;*
*He carried out his word, which He commanded long*
*ago...* ***(Lamentations 2:17)***

*I cry out to God Most High, to God who fulfills his*
*purpose for me.*
***(Psalms 57:2)***

*And we know that for those who love God all things*
*work together for good,        for those who are*
*called according to His purpose.*
***(Romans 8:28)***

# All The Doors Are Opened

All the door are open

But it takes faith to seize the moment.

Dare to be different! Dare to explore!

Dare to walk with confidence through the open door.

All the doors are open,

But you must protect your mind.

God is for you, and He's all you need.

To unlock the kingdom, your faith is the key.

All the doors are open,

But you must be at the place ordained for you.

If you dwell in the secret place of The Most High,

When you get tired, the angels of God

Will escort you through.

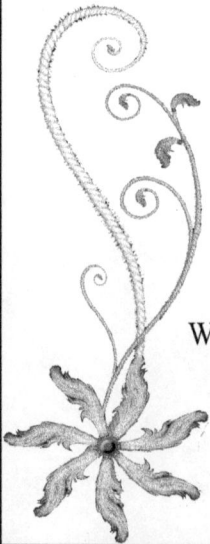

All the doors are open,

So cast the shadow of doubt away,

Reach for the prize! Continue to press!

Walk through the door. Go meet your success.

# Anointed for Purpose

You are anointed by The Almighty God,

To operate  the gifts, talents and abilities,

With which you have been entrusted...

Before the beginning of time.


The  anointing upon your life,

Enables you to…

Recognize potential,

See possibilities,

Fulfill your purpose.


Know! Your anointing is especially tailored for you!

Release your faith this moment.

Allow the anointing to manifest itself,

And to build your confidence.


*Jeremiah 29:11-14; 1John 2:20; Exodus 35:30;*

*Proverbs 29:18*

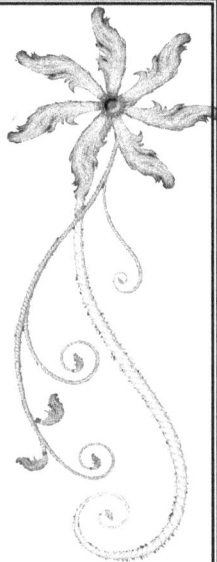

# Available

I am one person Lord,
Are You looking for one person?
A person who wants to serve You?
Are You looking for an individual,
An individual willing to follow You?

Lord I am humbling myself.
I am surrendering all to You,
Lord, You have used others in the past,
So I know You can use me too.

What do you want from me?
Show me through your word.
Where do you want me to go?
Show me and I will go for you.

My heart is ready.
My soul is yearning.
Whatever your plan is,
I long to fulfill it.
*(Isaiah 6:1-8)*

# Answering the Call of God

When my Father calls
My soul recognizes His voice.
My spirit answers and responds,
And my spirit, soul and body fulfill His demands.

When my Father calls,
He has called me to be the solution.
I am the advocate for His cause,
I am the voice of change and reason.

When my Father calls,
His cause supersedes everything in my life.
It gets my attention, time, and resources,
And I am transformed into an impact person.

When my Father calls,
I become a source for His deposition
My potential is realized,
And the resources I need, my Father supplies.

*((Mark 3:13; Nehemiah 1: 1-11;*
*Exodus 3: 1-10; Isaiah 51:3)*

# Believe It!

There is a cause,
That calls unto you.
Urging you to get involved,
To make a difference in the lives of men.

Let not the devil destroy your confidence,
Believe in who you are.
Believe in your God-given potential,
Believe that there's nothing too difficult for you to do.

There are spiritual forces holding people in mental captivity,
So God has empowered you,
To carry out His decree
To set His people free.

This is your set time for the favor of God.
You are endorsed, supported and equipped by Him.
It does not matter what the past holds,
You have the favor, mercy and covenant with
the Omnipotent One.

Profuse favor has been lavished unto you,
Continuously being poured out in excess.
God has made the way clear,
For what He has called you to do.

*(Mark 3:13; Exodus 5; Exodus 7;*
*Psalms 102: 13; Luke 4:18)*

# Called By God

I am that generation
Called and anointed by God.
The enemy may try to create doubt,
But I know I am a blessing,
Blessed by God and called by His Name.

I am that generation,
The generation that fears God.
The enemy may try to trick me,
But I know I'm a blessing,
Called to fulfill my God-given assignment on earth.

I am that generation
Divinely favored by the Almighty.
The enemy may try to distract me,
But I know I'm a blessing,
Called to worship God in spirit and in truth.

I am that generation,
Who received supernatural power,
Over everything on earth.
The enemy may try to influence my desires,
But I know I am a blessing,
Called to reflect God's word, love,
mercy, and grace supernaturally.

I am that generation,
Blessed and secured in God,
The enemy may try to disturb my peace
But I know I am a blessing,
Called to put my faith in God
and not to lean on my own understanding.

I am that generation,
Chosen and set apart for the service of God.
The enemy may try to entrap me,
But I know I am a blessing,
Called to a life of holiness,
Reflecting and perpetuating the character and nature of God.
*(1 Peter 2:11)*

## Chosen

Lord, You have chosen me
To be on Your team.
I vow to play my part,
To share the word,
And minister to touch men's heart.

Lord, I'm a pixel,
Compared to the vastness of the universe.
You are awesome in power and might,
Yet, You have chosen me to help
With the good fight.

Lord, it's hard for my mind to conceive
The trust You've placed in me.
You have the entire world to choose from,
Yet, You have chosen me.

## Compelled

There's a burden upon my heart,
For the children of this land.
I have been called to serve them,
And to help them in whatever way I can.

The Lord has compelled me
To make a difference in this world,
I cannot sit still and rest
It's time for me to take a stand,
And employ my very best.

My mind is tormented by the pain I feel,
Compelling me to take action.
I have my assignment to complete,
It's more than a mental commitment,
It requires the use of my eyes, hands and feet.

God has compelled me to make a difference
And the resources He'll provide.
Amidst the tears and heartaches,
I will not be distracted.

# Created for Success

God has created me for one thing.
I was designed for success!
When God made me,
He made me to accomplish
The purpose for which I was fashioned,
I was created for success!


The Almighty gave me the ability
To look at life's challenges,
Not with eyes focused on the temporary
But through the eyes of faith.

The path of life I have taken,
Is leading me towards the objective for which
I was molded…

I was designed for…
Uncompromising,
Unsurpassed
SUCCESS!

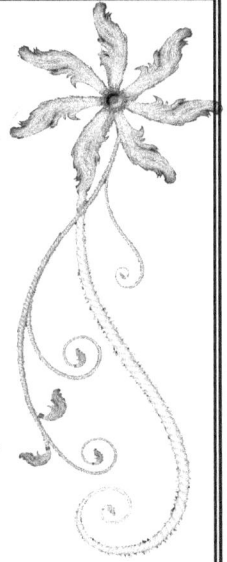

# Discovering Your Cause

God needs you to answer your cause.
There's no one to complete your assignment.
It will not get done, unless you step in,
To do your part, in this world plagued with sin.

You are the catalyst for the change men need.
You are the solution, recruited to intervene.
It takes one person,
Not an entire nation.
So step out in faith.
Stop procrastinating!

You are yeast
creating change gradually.
Your efforts is not temporary.
It will be lasting.
God has sown Himself into you through His Word,
So you can be the blessing, in the dough of the world.

Be not concerned with resources you lack.
Be obedient to God…
He has your back!
You are purposefully and uniquely designed
With talents, gifts and skills
To complete the task …
For which you've been assigned.

*Matthew 13:33; Ephesians 1:26; 1Kings 17*

# Desire

I want to see You, Jesus.
I'm anticipating Your impact on me.
I understand Zaccheus' desire,
And the reason he climbed the tree.

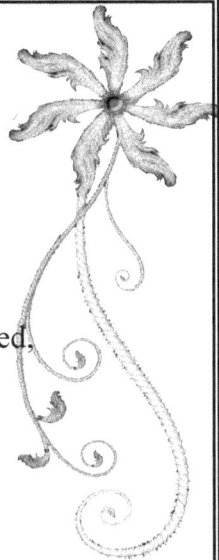

I want to touch You Jesus,
I know You can change me.
I understand the yearning of the woman, who bled,
And the reason she held unto You.

I want to experience You, Jesus.
I know You can set me free.
I understand the lepers' pain and anxiety
And the reasons they called out to Thee.

I want to hear You, Jesus.
I know You can restore me.
I understand the longing of the blind man,
And the reason he yelled above the crowd.

I want to praise You Jesus.
I know You love me.
I understand the reason You died on the cross,
And the reason You've forgiven me.

*(Luke 19)*

35

# Destiny Awaits!

Your level of sight for your destiny,
Must extend further…
Further than your experiences.
It must extend further…
Further than your current situation.
Your destiny must be based on your vision,
And your vision steadfastly based
Upon the word of God.

Regardless of what you see on the outside,
Regardless of what you currently believe,
Regardless of words of negativity spoken against you,
Your  success is waiting on the inside of you!
Your destiny is awaiting its birth,
It's waiting for you to impact nations of the earth.

Allow the Omnipotent One to work in your heart,
Cause that's the place where your vision is born.
He will transform your entire system
Causing you to see your destiny,
From conception to manifestation.

# Empty

I am like an empty cup without You,
Longing to fulfill my purpose.
Fill my cup Lord,
With Your holy presence and goodness,
So I may be a vessel of honor for You.


Outside I may be beautify adorn,
But on the inside I'm lacking.
My heart and mind are waiting,
Longing to be filled by You.


Fill me Lord,
Let me be empty no more.
In my heart I long for You to abide.
Come into my heart,
So I may be filled with Your love, peace and joy.

# Give Me Your Heart Lord

Give me Your heart Lord,
A heart filled with love and compassion
For the lost and weary.

Give me Your heart Lord,
A heart that remains grounded and steadfast,
Regardless of life's circumstances.

Give me Your heart Lord,
A heart that loves,
Even when flesh does not want to.

Give me Your heart Lord,
A heart that hungers
And thirst after righteousness.

Give me your heart Lord,
A heart that knows and understands
The spiritual warfare that's raging over my soul.

Give me Your heart Lord,
A heart that knows the Heavenly Father,
And knows and hears his voice.

Give me your heart Lord,
A heart that loves unconditionally,
Extended even to those who hurt and persecute me

Give me your heart Lord,
A heart that is moved to action
To search for and reach those who are longing.

Give me your heart Lord,
A heart that believes and obeys.
A heart that lives the word of God.

# Go!

Go! Go and tell the world,
About the love of Jesus Christ.
Go and share the good news,
To people both near and far.

Be not ashamed to spread the Gospel,
It is good news to all.
The world can be better,
If we trust and obey the Lord.

People are yearning for a purpose
Waiting for their lives to change.
We can fill that void and longing,
By sharing the love of Christ.

Go! Go and tell the world,
About the love of Jesus Christ.
Go and share the good news,
To people both near and far.

*(Romans 1:6 ; 2 Corinthians 5:17)*

# God's Doing a New Thing

Satan wants you connected to the mistakes of your past,
So you'll be trapped, enslaved, condemned,
Unable to dream dreams that will last.
He tries to get you focused on former things,
So you won't realize, that in you God's doing a new thing.

Pride of past achievement will cause loss of momentum,
Creating complacency, stagnation, and destruction within.
It will paralyze your dream and creativity,
Destroying self-concept, self-image and self-identity.
But hope is not lost, cause in you God's doing a new thing.

Laced with lies is the tendency to compare,
Your life with others and that which you hold dear.
It's the plan of the devil to obscure your vision,
With fear, curses, worry and paranoia
But hope is not lost, cause in you God's doing a new thing.

Let not the pressure cause you to shift,
From the mission you've been called to accomplish.
Obstacles will manifest themselves in various ways,
But hope is not lost, cause God is doing a new thing...
In you today.

*Isaiah 43:18-19; Micah 2:20; Galatians 3:13-14;*
*1 Samuels2; 2Corinthians 10:12*

# It Will Be Done

Help me to hear Your voice Lord,
As I listen and read Your word.
Help me to listen to Your voice,
As You direct my path.


Whatever you want me to do,
I will do it!
Where ever you want me to go,
I will go for you.
Whomsoever you want me to speak to
I will speak to him or her.
Whenever you want me to start,
I will begin my journey.


Help me to hear Your voice Lord,
And help me to listen.


*(Isaiah 6; Jeremiah 1)*

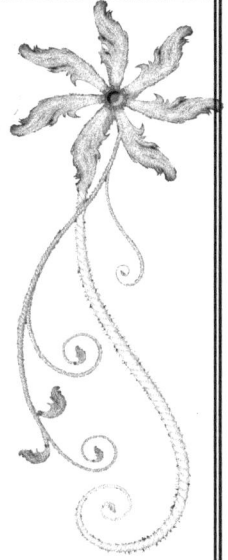

# Journey of Faith

Lord, help me not to lose faith,
When catastrophe is plaguing my life.
Help me to hold unto The Truth,
Regardless of my current situation.

Lord, when my eyes are searching for proof
And I cannot see it in the flesh,
Let me remember to believe, when evidence seems lacking
And the outcome I naturally cannot see.

Lord, You have called me to trust You,
Help me along the journey of faith,
To embrace then dismiss my doubts
As you grant me courage each step I take.

Lord, help me to look beyond the pain,
And the failures of a carnal mind.
Help me to keep my eyes on You,
Regardless of the problems I face.

# Knowing

Danger lurks around the corner,
But my deliverer is near.
Trouble lingers outside my door,
Yet I need not live in fear!

I put my trust in Jesus
My confidence is in the Lord.
It matters not what comes my way,
I know I am safe and protected in Christ.

**(Psalms 23)**

# My Soul, Wake Up!

My soul, my soul,
Why are you quiet within me?
Why do you remain still,
Oblivious to the havocs of sin?

My soul, my soul,
Why aren't you screaming?
Why are you not commanding my body,
To get busy for our King?

My soul, my soul,
Align with my spiritual man.
Let my mind, will and emotion
Be subjected to the will of God.

My soul, my soul
The Spirit of God is beckoning,
My spiritual man is answering,
Be awake, and join in!

# Needing God

Lord, when I am feeling overwhelmed,
And do not know what to do,
Remind me that You are in control,
And I should put my trust in You.

When the world seems to be spinning,
And life seems to be moving too fast,
Help me to stop and remember,
That You are my deliverer and Savior.

When the demands of work and family
Makes me feel like I'm about to break,
Give me Your strength to endure,
Guard and guide my thoughts each step I take.

# Obedience

Fear and impatience may hinder my obedience,
Causing me to step away…
Away from Your perfect plan for me.
My disobedience hampers my success
And the favor you have ordained for me.


Lord, I long to be obedient unto thee.
Help me! Break my will!
Let me see me through Your eyes
And the hope and joy that obedience brings.


Let me not justify nor rationalize my actions,
Cause partial obedience is not what You want from me.
Take me back to following You.
Extend your grace and mercy one more time towards me.

Speak to me Lord, I will obey You.
Partial obedience is not what You from me,
So I am recommitting my all –
My mind, my emotion and my will, I pledge to You.

*(Story of Samson ; Isaiah 1:19)*

# On Bended Knees

Lord, on bended knees
I bow before thee
Thanking You for the price
You paid for me upon the cross.

I offer my heart to You,
In these uncertain times,
Because regardless of what the future holds,
You hold me close and will never let me go.

On bended knees,
I respond to Your call,
Inviting you to be Lord of my life,
From now until eternity.

# Ravished for Righteousness

There's a burning fire within me,
Is like a raging furnace.
It is flaming and unstoppable,
It can only be contained, if me You embrace.

The cry of my soul, is stronger than I imagined.
It rings within my being constantly.
Waking me at nights, it's impossible to ignore.
Until my soul ignites for service,
This longing I'll continue to endure.

I am hungry and thirsty for You.
Ravished. I purpose to tarry.
I will call and wait upon You.
Until this insatiable appetite is fed,
I simply cannot led You go.

## Remove Me Lord

Lord, I am Yours from now until eternity.
Remove me out of the way
So I may magnify Your Precious, Holy Name.

Father I am an instrument, created to be used by You.
Remove me out of the way,
So Your will can take effect,
And I may kneel at the feet of Jesus Christ.

Lord I know my life is in Your hands,
And you have a cause for me to embrace.
Remove me out of the way,
So I may walk in Your will for me, and fulfill my ordained destiny.

Remove me out of the way,
Lord, please remove me out of my way,
Remove me Lord, so I may find myself in You.

## Roam Lord, Roam

Father, roam around in my life.
This is my prayer today.
Wander throughout every area
Challenge me to action I pray.
Let me hear You!
Let me see You!
Let me feel Your presence.

Roam around in my heart Lord,
Stir and rekindle my being.
Let me be uncomfortable with sitting still,
Show me where I am lacking
Reveal me to me,
Then let me see me through Your eyes,
As the precious child of a King.

## Set Free

No one can convict me,
Except for the Lord.
No one can see my every deed,
Or the thoughts I hold in my heart.

I confess to You Lord,
That I long to be free.
Help me to escape the thoughts
That are trying to sneer me.

I look to the power of the cross,
For cleansing and forgiveness.
I know that through your blood,
I am delivered and set free.

*(Mark 5:1)*

## Stop and Reflect

Be now informed!
Be aware and acknowledge.

Your passion in life,
Is tied to your purpose.

Seek no longer for joy and fulfillment.

Recognize God's Hands upon your life.

Success is already ordained for you.

Stop!

Reflect!

Allow God Almighty to use you.

# Sense of Urgency

I am a believer,
Commissioned by the Lord,
To be in action,
For the King of Kings.

There's a sense of urgency
Propelling me to go on.
Souls are being drawn to hell,
Unless the truth of Jesus I tell.

I cannot sit still!
More than prayer is required.
Souls are dying,
People are crying,
Unless they encounter the Risen Christ,
They won't know there's more to life,
Than they're currently experiencing.

I am a believer,
Commissioned by the Lord,
To be in action,
For the King of Kings.

*Matthew 13; Acts 16: 11– 24; Acts 16: 25– 31*

# Step Away From Negativity

Give yourself permission
To step away from negativity
And from people who will feed you doubt.

Unbelief will hinder your success,
And your walk with Almighty God.
Do not give up on your blessing,
And the promises of God.
Give yourself permission…

Nothing is impossible with God!
You were created and structured for your journey,
All the resources you need are yours,
If you trust and believe.
Give yourself permission…

God made you special for Him.
You're a vessel, an instrument designed to be used.
It matters not where you came from,
It's who you are, when you apply the word of God.
Give yourself permission…

God will strengthen you
As you seek and put Him first.
He has something special for you to do,
He will never leave nor forsake you,
Remember, you have a purpose to fulfill,
With you, God is not through.

I will give myself permission,
To step away from negativity,
And from people who will feed me doubt!

*(Matthew 14: 22-23; Job 13:15; Psalms 8: 1-9;
1Timothy 1: 12-14)*

# The End Time

I think about the end times
And what Your Word proclaims.
I know that the end is coming,
When we'll all stand before Your throne.


I know I will not know the moment,
When You'll return to earth.
But I know it will be a day of reckoning
Whether or not we believe in the second birth.


My mind struggles to fully understand,
The nature of the end days' plan.
But I fully believe in the rapture
And the forgiveness and redemption of man.


*(1 Thessalonians 5; Genesis 1: 3 – 4)*

# The Challenge to Forgive

My responsibility is to forgive,
Not to hold unto grudges.
To let go of the desire for revenge,
To replace hate with love and goodness.


Sometimes it is hard,
And the desire to forgive is missing.
It is so easy to harbor hate when the pain goes deep.
Oftentimes it's extremely difficult, to just let it go.


Sometimes the anger stays and fosters
And the manifestation is destructive.
Confronting conflict may be undesirable of me
But the longer I wait, the harder it gets to forgive.


Lord, I commit to You today
To rise above my human nature.
So although the hurt burrows deep,
Although it is difficult
Although my sinful nature resists, I'll replace love with hate.

And the mercy, grace and forgiveness You're extending to me
With Your help, I will extend to others the same courtesy.

## Through the Blood

God has created everyone,
As a very special person.
Regardless of one's status in life,
We are all the same in God's eyes.

God created us in His image,
Wrapped in compassion and love.
He knew us before we were born,
Our destiny ordained, from the beginning of time.

Daily we're extended unconditional love,
A constant reminder to come home God.
Although we were born in sin and shame,
Through the blood of Jesus Christ,
We stand before God loved, forgiven and without blame.

## Unworthy

Lord, I feel unworthy
To stand before You.
I feel unworthy Lord,
To call upon Your name.

I am silent before You.
Silent in my desires,
Silent as I acknowledge,
Your awesome power and grace.

Lord, I humble myself.
On bended knees I surrender.
I surrender my dismissive attitude,
And my clouded judgment.

Lord, I feel unworthy,
Yet You love me.
I feel unworthy,
Yet You have forgiven me.
I feel unworthy, Lord
Yet with open arms You embrace me.

You have removed the feeling of worthlessness
Replacing it with love, mercy and righteousness.

# War of Deception

The human body is uniquely designed,
Created in the image and likeness of God.
Deposited inside you is a portion of the King,
His omniscience and omnipotence,
He planted within.

Satan is on a war path, trying to attack your mind.
To get you absorbed, focused on self and time.
His weapons of intimidation and complacency he launches,
Wanting you to return to the grave,
Without fulfilling your vision.

The devil is on a rampage, to block your mind.
Desiring to thwart your vision, by making you blind.
He wants to separate you from the thoughts of God,
By tempting you to live in habitual sin.

The devil wants you to accept the status quo,
To live void of progress, unsure of where to go.
He tries to burden you with what your eyes see,
Causing you to doubt the place of your destiny.

*(2 Corinthians 4:3-4; Ephesians 4:23;*
*Deuteronomy 28:1; Ezekiel 18:4 )*

# What Time is it?

This is not the time for relaxation.
This is not the time for complacency.
This is not the time for inaction.
The harvest is ripe, and God is calling.

Have you worked for God lately?
Have you tried to reach one soul?
What about your neighbor?
Have you witnessed to them? Prayed for them?
Or are you too busy being heaven-bound?

This is your day of reckoning,
Look away. Look down. The words will linger.
Your conscience has been pricked.
You'll be inactive no more.
The time is now.
God's people are waiting.
Get up. Get out. Do your part.
What time is it?
It's time to do your part.

. . . . . . . . . . . . . . . . . . . . . . . . . . . . . . . . . .

# Why Wait?

What am I waiting for,
To give my all to You?
Why do I delay my commitment,
When Your Word is clearly true?

What am I waiting for,
To turn away from sin?
Why am I not repenting,
When that's all You're asking?

What am waiting for,
When You've extended grace towards me?
Why am I not loving you ,
And embracing all You want me to be?

What am I waiting for?
What am I waiting for?
What am I waiting for,
To give my all to you?

# Winning the Blame Game

Immerse yourself in the word of God,
And let God use you for His glory!
Let go of the guilt and shame.
The time is now to stop the blame!


Regardless of what you went through
Let it go! It's not your fault!
Be not crippled by your past.
Pretend no more, take off the mask.


Realize that God is in control.
He has prepared you,
Like jewels made of gold
To go through the fire
So your purpose, you will behold.


Align your passion with your purpose.
Step into your victory!
Let go of the blame!
You're a winner...
Designed to keep on winning the blame game.

*(John 9:3)*

# Word of Blessing

A blessing was pronounced upon me
A moment I'll cherish forever.
I understand what God has granted,
And the promises He made to me.

I am blessed to be a blessing,
To share what God has done.
I have been raised up in this time,
Because of the plan God has for me.

I am anointed, thus protected,
By the grace of Almighty God.
It matters not where I came from,
But where and who I am in God.

*(Duet. 6: 1-9; 11 Samuel 23:1 – 5)*

# You Are Real

You could have remained hidden.
You could have stayed in the shadows,
Instead You chose to reveal Yourself to me.

You have expressed Yourself to me
Through nature…
Through my conscience…
And throughout history.
Constantly I am reminded, Father
That You exist and You are real.

My eyes are opened to the truth,
The scriptures have drawn me closer to You.
Jesus Christ Your Begotten Son,
Through His blood has reconciled me unto you.

You have called me by name,
To have a relationship with you,
Through your son Jesus Christ, I have been set free.

*(Hebrews 1: 1-3)*

# Your Purpose

There is no failure
When God is glorified.
You have been called,
Ordained for a purpose in this world.
Seek to know why you were created,
And start living in the will and plan of God.

Once you find your purpose,
Your life will never be the same.
The gifts and talents you need to be successful,
Are already within you.

Let your gifts and talents not lie dormant any longer.
Accept them!
Activate them!
And fulfill your purpose in grace,
Through Christ Jesus who strengthens you.

*(Philippians 3:12; Proverbs 19: 21; Jeremiah 1: 4-5)*

# Your Word

Lord, your word protects me
Financial advice through Proverbs You share.
Worry and stress sometimes consume me,
My heart pounds so fast,
It seems it will burst from my chest.

In Philippians You remind me,
Not to be anxious about today.
Through Colossians You declare,
Whatever I do, I should do it to the best of my ability.

I know faith without work is dead,
So build my faith I pray.
Then strengthen both spiritual and physical man
So I may handle whatever comes my way.

# Praise

*Praise the Lord! I will give thanks to the Lord with my whole heart...*
**(Psalms 111:1)**

*Praise the Lord!*
*Blessed is the man who fears the Lord, who greatly delights in His commandments!*
**(Psalms 112:1)**

*The Lord is my strength and my song, and He has become my salvation; this is my God and I will praise Him, my father's God, and I will exalt Him.*
**(Exodus 15:2)**

*He is your praise. He is your God, who has done for you these great and terrifying things that your eyes have seen.*
**(Deuteronomy 10:21)**

*I call upon the Lord, who is worthy to be praised, and I am saved from my enemies.*
**(2 Samuel 22:4)**

*Great is the Lord and greatly to be praised in the city of our God!*
**(Psalms 48:1)**

*O Lord, you are my God; I will exalt you; I will praise your name, for you have done wonderful things, plans formed of old, faithful and sure.*
**(Isaiah 25:1)**

*Heal me, O Lord, and I shall be healed; save me, and I shall be saved, for You are my praise.*
**(Jeremiah 17:14)**

*Praise the Lord! Oh give thanks to the Lord for He is good, for His steadfast love endures forever!*
**(Psalms 106)**

*O Lord My God, You are Very Great. Psalms 104*
*Tell of All His Wonderful Works (Psalms 105)*
*Who is like the Lord our God! (Psalms 113*

# Abba Father

Abba Father, Resider of Heaven,
Hallelujah to your precious name.
Your Shekina Glory swaddles me,
And your favor surrounds me like a shield.

Every morning when I rise,
I'm reminded that I am the apple of Your eyes.
I can feel Your warm and gentle embrace,
Like the soft kiss of a beautiful spring breeze upon my face.

Like a parched field
Exposed to the scorching summer's heat,
My soul awaits an abundant outpouring of Your Spirit,
Cause the hunger and thirst that I feel
Can only be satisfied in You,
My Jehovah Jireh, who always provide.

Unlike the trees in Autumn
Whose leaves change and fall to the ground,
Ancient of Days, You change not!
In You, no wavering can be found.

On a bright crisp winter morning,
When wild wind whistles in my ears,
I can still hear Your calm and reassuring voice,
Beckoning me to draw closer, because You are near.

# All I Need Is You Lord

Lord, there are no surprises with You.
Each day, each moment, You already know.
From the beginning of time,
You have ordained my life,
So today, I live in hope because of You.


Lord, You desire to bless my life,
From now until eternity.
Above all else, You want my life to prosper,
As my soul prospers in You.


Lord, You have my best interest at heart,
Regardless of the situations I face.
Whether joys, trials or tribulations,
I know You will always love me.


Lord, you preserve me,
Cause in You, do I put my trust.
Nothing can disturb my'peace,
Cause my refuge and strength is in You,
God of the Universe.

*(Psalms 2:7; Psalms 4:3; Psalms 9: 9-11; Psalms 16)*

# Already Done Through Jesus Christ

Justification is already done,
Through the precious blood of Jesus Christ.
There's nothing for me to do,
Except to trust and love You.

Sanctification I obtained  by grace,
To set myself apart for Thee,
To allow You to live in my heart,
And to trust You in my daily walk.

Glorification is yet to come,
The day I reunite with You.
Today I live each moment,
With the knowledge of that glorious day.

*(Romans 4:25; Exodus 31:13; John 17:17;
John 17:1John 12:28; Psalms 8:5)*

## Barrier-Breaking Book — The Holy Bible

People tried to convince me
That I couldn't be who I wanted to be.
For years I embraced negativity,
Believing it reflected the true me.

I was ignored and dismissed,
Because of where I was born.
Ostracized, belittled and condemned
Because of what people see,
When they take a moment to glance towards me.

For years I struggled with self-confidence,
Feeling overwhelmed and entrapped,
I thought there was no escaping the past,
And what society dictated would last.

Out of desperation and desolation
I proved the world wrong!
I was given a copy of my favorite book,
And learned the truth
About who I am and where I belong.

**(Genesis 1:26;-27;
Jeremiah 1:5; Isaiah 18-19 & 25;
2Timothy 3:16-17)**

# Benevolent King and Father

Father, You are the benevolent King,
Who loves and cares for me.
You get your glory and praise,
When I'm blessed and testify of your grace.


Father, You never change,
Your mercy is everlasting.
You're omnipotent and omniscient,
Worthy to be praised!


The earth belongs to You,
And everything in it.
So I lift my voice and shout,
Halleluiah to You, King of Kings.

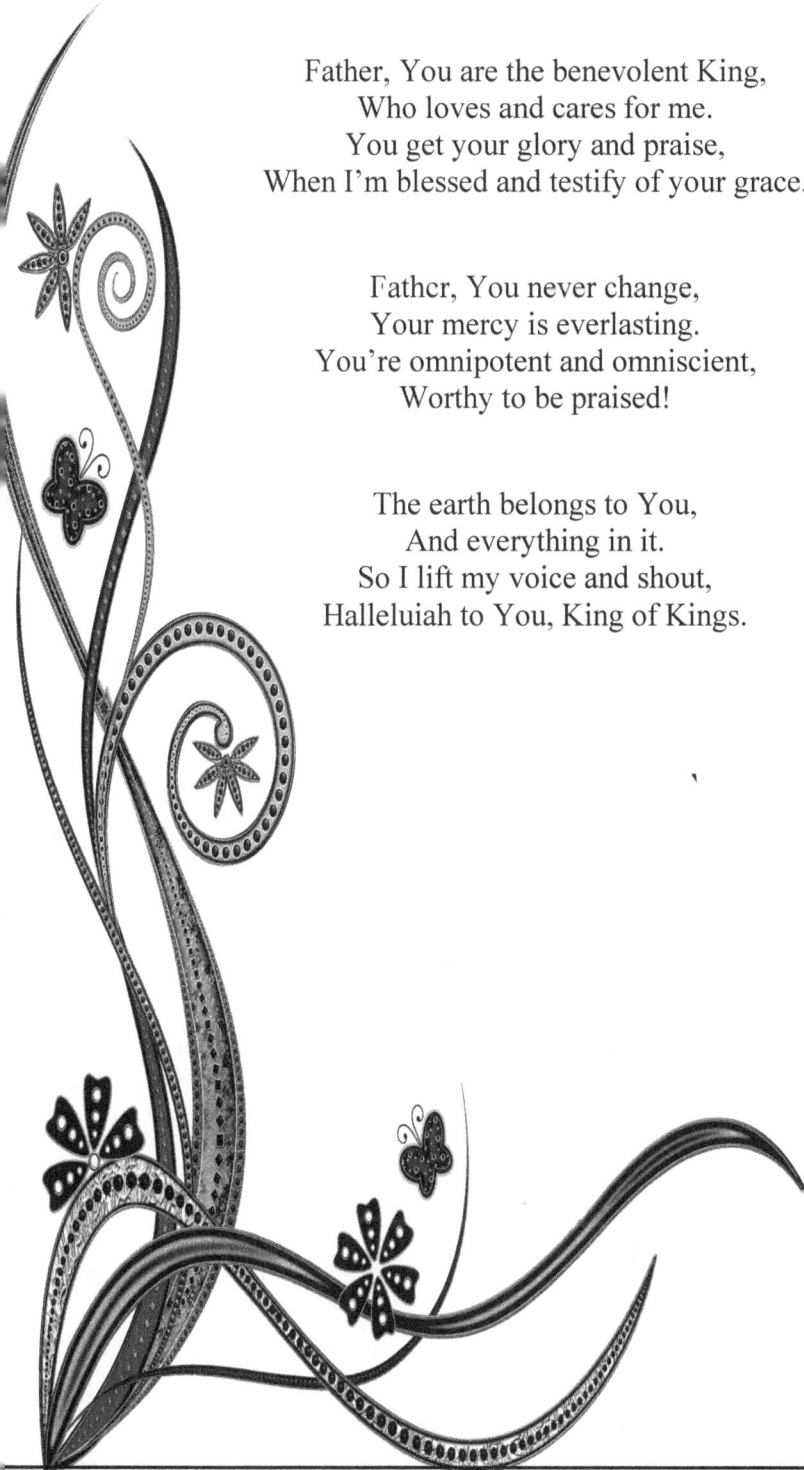

# Because of You, I Am

Because of You,
I can stand and face the problems of this land.
Because of You,
I know all my needs and desires are satisfied,
Because of You,
I can dream far beyond my imagination.
Because of You…

Because of You,
I have a plan and purpose for my life,
Because of You,
I have grace sufficient for every situation,
Because of You,
I have the Holy Spirit, I'm never alone.
Because of You…

Because of You,
I'm blessed and favored by the Omnipotent One,
Because of You,
My sins are forgiven and forgotten too,
Because of You,
I can resist the devil and he'll flee from me,

Because of You…

*(1 Cor. 10:13; 2 Cor. 4:18; 1 Cor. 1:30; 2 Cor. 10: 3-5)*
*(Psalms 37:23; 2Corinthians. 12:9; Philippians. 4:7)*
*(Jeremiah 31:33; Psalms 34: 19)*

# Breakthrough

Like Jacob who held on,
Refusing to let go,
I will cling to You Jesus,
Until I experience my breakthrough.


Like Job who endured,
Refusing to give in,
I will believe for my breakthrough,
I will not quit, because I know I will win.


Like Ruth who journeyed to a distant land,
Refusing to stay behind,
I will follow You Jesus,
Until my breakthrough is realized.


Like Shadrach, Meshach and Abendego,
Who refused to bow down,
I will rest assured in You Jesus,
Until my breakthrough is done.


Like the little shepherd boy,
Who refused to be dismayed,
I will look to You Jesus,
Because my breakthrough is on its way.

*(Genesis 32; 24-28; Job 13:15; Ruth 1:16-17;*
*Daniel 3:16– 26; 1 Samuel 17; 44-49*

# Child of The Light

I am a child of The Light,
Created in the image and likeness of God!
My joy is not based on what is happening
But cemented in Jesus Christ the Lord.


I am a child of The Light,
No longer subjected to condemnation.
My sins and iniquities are all forgiven,
My mind has been renewed
Through the blood of Jesus Christ.


I am a child of The Light,
Granted an enormous amount of grace.
I am blessed and highly favored
All my needs are met and surpassed
Since the completed work of Jesus, I embrace.

# God Almighty

I will praise you always, Most High God.
My lips shall never be still.
From the moment I rise each morning,
My God, my strength, to you my heart will sing.

You are El Shaddai, God Almighty.
You reign for ever as King of kings,
You arc forever the same, clothed in majesty.
Adonai, My Lord I give you everything.

Oh Omnipotent One, all things are possible for You.
When You speak , Your words take form,
Accomplishing that which You inspire.
Elohim, My Creator, You are my soul's desire.

Jehovah Jireh, My Provider,
You supply all my needs,
According to Your riches in glory.
Your grace is sufficient  and everlasting,
So my spirit, soul and body,
Join forces in thanksgiving.

# God's Committed To Me

God is committed to leading me.
But I must dare to dream.
Dream beyond my past.
Dream beyond my present.
Dream beyond my perceived potential.

God is committed to my success.
Bust I must dare to have a vision.
Vision transforms the unknown.
Vision eradicates problems.
Vision provides direction, inspiration and solution.

God is committed to my purpose,
But  I must align it with His will.
His will directs my steps.
His will guides my thoughts.
His will propels me to action
When self  wishes not to go on.

*Proverbs 29:18; Proverbs 19:21;*
*Daniel 1; Exodus 32:25*   `

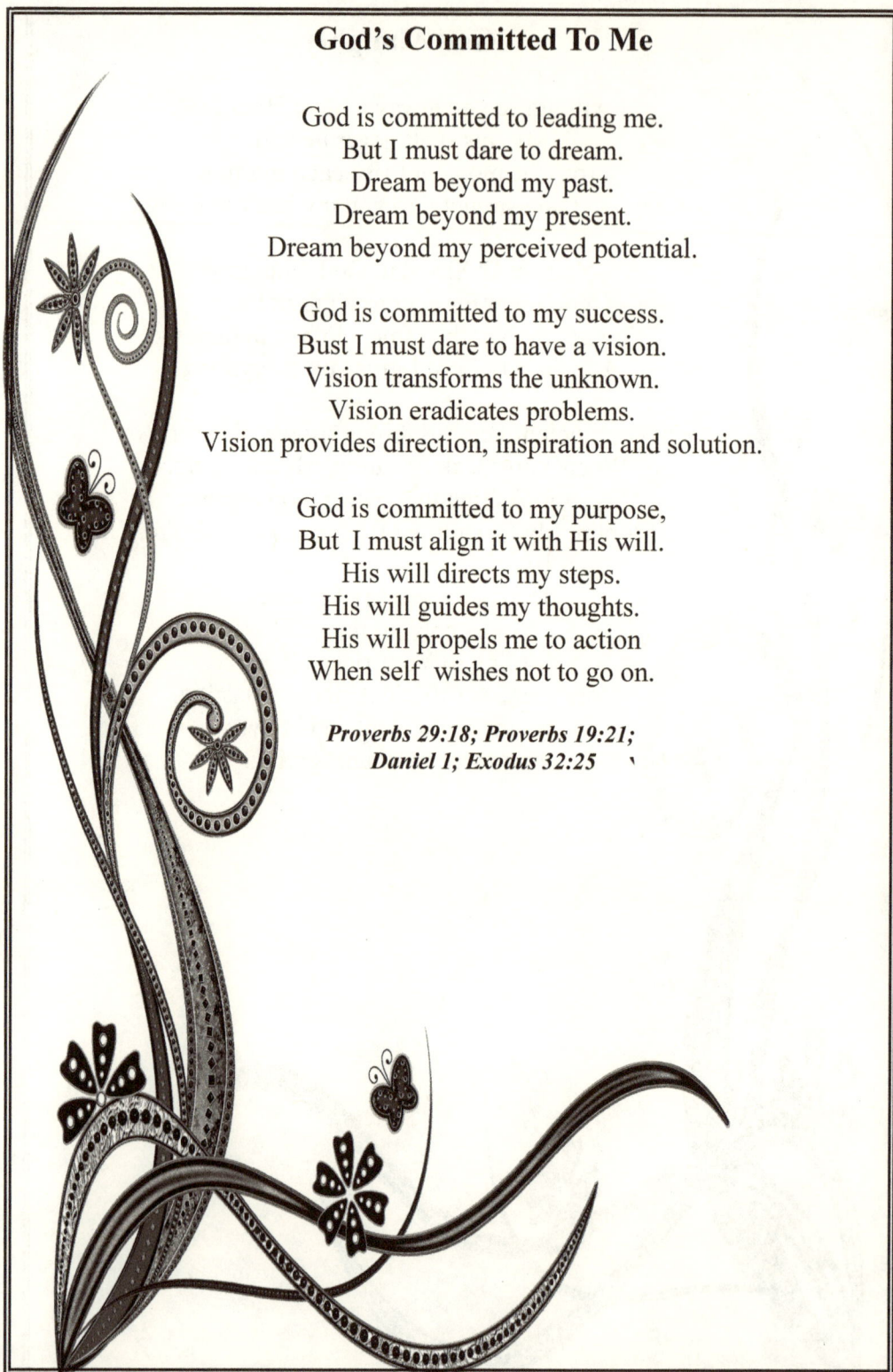

# Come Magnify the Lord With Me

Come magnify the Lord with me,
Come glorify the Lord with me,
In God's presence,
Salvation is free!
He's the rock, on which I stand.
He's the Lord, the great I AM.
When I'm feeling down,
God is lifting me.


Come magnify the Lord with me,
Come glorify the Lord with me,
In God's presence,
Salvation is free!
He has a purpose for my life,
My destiny he ordained before birth,
If I trust and obey,
I'll live in victory.


Come magnify the Lord with me,
Come glorify the Lord with me,
In God's presence,
Salvation is free!
In God's presence,
That's where I want to be.
In God's presence, there's room for you and me.
In God's presence, I'll go on bended knees.
In God's presence, salvation is free.

# Covenant—God

God is a Covenant-God,
He desires to bless you,
And make you prosperous
Even as your soul prospers in Him.

God is a Covenant-God,
So anchor yourself in His word.
His promises are true,
And to that which He has committed,
He'll follow through.

God is a Covenant-God,
So embrace the relationship
The blood has cemented for you.
When life gets complicated,
He's willing and able to go above and beyond,
To make a way out for you.

*(Deuteronomy 28: 1-8; Genesis 15: 1-18)*

## Creator of Heaven and Earth

Creator of heaven and earth,
My heart sings your praise.
From the moment I awake,
Your name will be glorified.

There is nothing created without You.
Your love is plastered all over the earth.
From the green grass that hugs the ground,
To the highest mountain range.

From the sweet fragrance of a rose petal.
To planets spinning in place in space.
Creation testifies of your beauty,
And its intricate details
boasts your splendor and majesty.

## Darkness - Displaced By Light

Have you ever felt alone,
Yet you were surrounded by family and friends?
Have you ever felt void and empty,
Yet you have a list of things to get done?

Have you ever trusted a friend,
Yet you were betrayed and let down?
Take a moment and reflect,
Have you trusted God yet?

In this world surrounded by darkness,
The Light of the world has come.
He will lead you to a better place,
If you will  reach for His outstretched hand.

Darkness may surround you temporarily,
And overpowers you with fight,
But if you will hold on and not quit
You'll see  it displaced by The Light.

## Disappointment

What is disappointment,
But my reaction to the facts?
There are things I'll be able to change,
And others I will not.

Why be disappointed,
When life takes an unexpected turn?
There are lessons I need to learn,
And experiences I need not have.

To be or not be disappointed,
Is a choice for me to make,
I'll face the truth with faith,
Grounded and assured by the word of God.

71

# Father-God

Father-God, you are omniscient,
Nothing is hidden form You.
You know my innermost thoughts and desires,
And wherever I go, there You'll be too!

Father-God, you are jealous for me.
You desire a heart full of praise.
And will eradicate all distractions,
So I will humbly seek Your face.

Father-God, you are patient and kind,
Your mercies are renewed every morning.
With an outstretched hand dripping with love,
You await the day when I seek You first,
Instead of relying on the wisdom of man.

Father-God, you are worthy of all praise.
You are omnipresent, dwelling in every space.
Your eyes behold the evil and the good of this land,
Yet you desire to communicate with man,
Providing peace that defies understanding
in this turbulent land.

# Feasting on the Word

I eat and drink,
Because I hunger and I thirst after Your righteousness.
I consume thy word daily,
Because of my longing for You.

I drink from You,
And feed upon You
Cause You are power,
And without You, I'm destined for a life plagued with failure.

I eat and remember Your body,
That was broken for me.
I drink and remember Your blood,
That You shed for me.

I eat and drink You, Lord
And welcome You in,
As You forgive and redeem me
And make me free from sin.
( Matthew 5:6; Matthew 6:33; John 6: 53 – 59)

# Forgive Me, Lord

Lord forgive me,
When I get frustrated,
Because my timetable for my life
Is not being fulfilled according to my time.

Lord forgive me
When I get discouraged,
Because my perceived moment of success,
Is being put on hold.

Lord, please forgive me,
When I'm doubtful
Because what I think ought to be,
Is not what You want for me.

Lord, please forgive me,
When I fail to ask for forgiveness,
Because pride or ignorance,
Prevents me from seeing the truth.

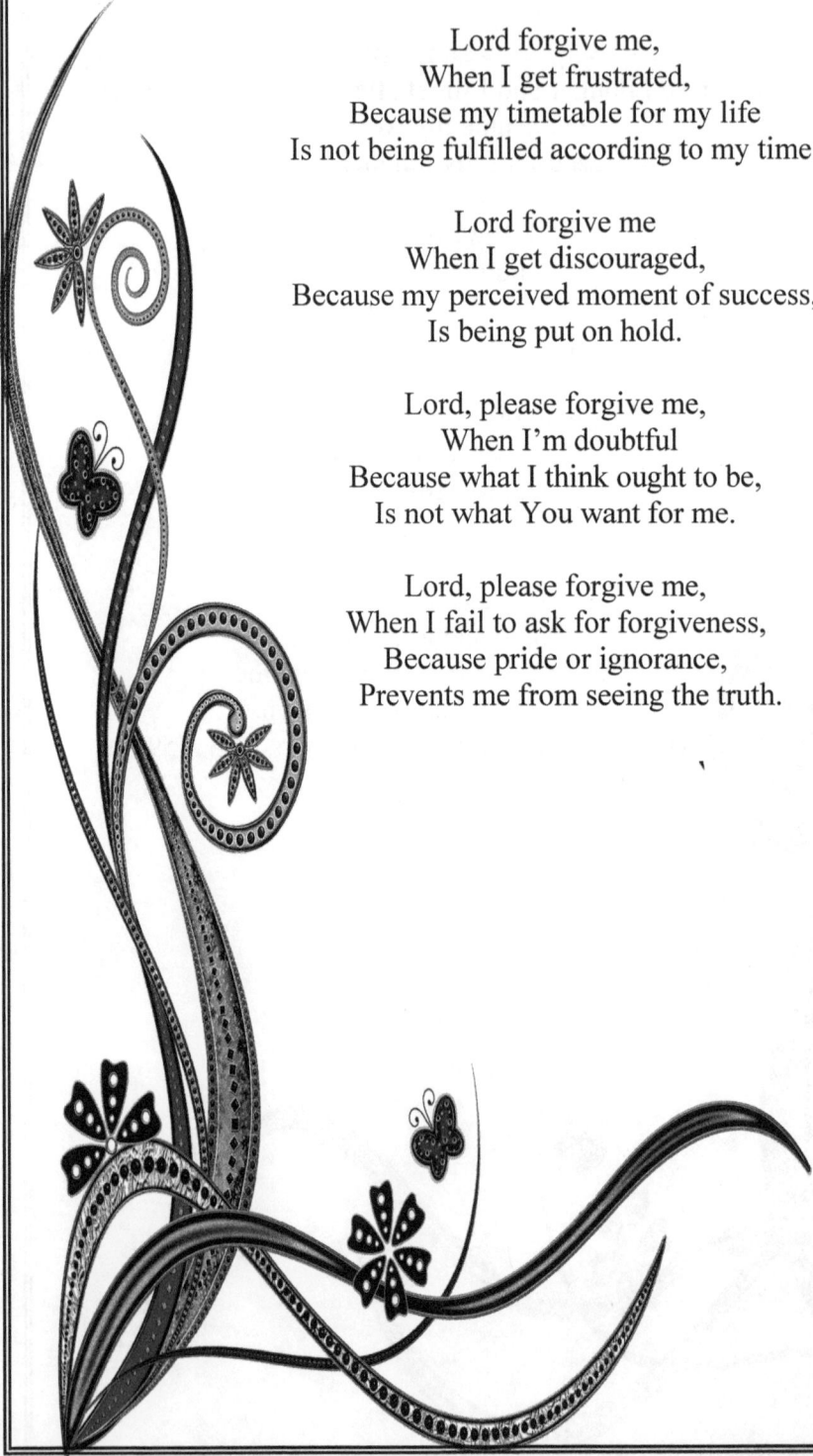

# God's Beauty

Lord, Your beauty far surpasses my imagination.
How magnificent You are!
I get excited thinking about Your Splendor,
But my mind fails to fully visualize Thee,
And I'm left to wonder
As Your majestic nature I consider.

In my humanity I rely on nature,
To grasp a glimpse of Your glorious being.
The whole earth is full of Your glory,
Thank you for revealing this to me.

*(Isaiah 8: 1-4)*

# God

God cannot be defined,
By humans' mind and understanding.
He cannot be confined
To our limitations.

God's love cannot be explained,
It cannot be surpassed,
It cannot be depleted.
It is, because He is.

# God's Compassion

Father, Your compassion gives me courage
In the midst of life's disappointments.
Your compassion sees me through,
Because You hold me
When I'm too weak to hold unto You.

Your compassion restores my faith,
And my desire to live for You.
Your compassion comforts me,
Cause you are the kind, caring, Father
Who loves me unconditionally.

Your compassion frees me,
From the mistakes of my past
Your compassion provides second chances
Enough to give me hope that lasts.

Your compassion is abundant,
Sufficient for life's journey.
Your compassion is endless,
Such revelation leaves me speechless.

# God's Love

God's love forgives me.
God's love accepts me.
God's love redeems me.
God is a God of Love.

God's love provides for me.
God's love heals me.
God's love protects me.
God is a God of Love.

God's love shields me.
God's love keeps me.
God's love envelops me.
God is God of Love.

God's love guides me.
God's love directs me.
God's love challenges me.
God is a God of Love.

# Grace Will See Me Through

Your grace has granted me peace.
Your favor, You've extended towards me.
Lord, I deserved nothing,
Yet You've chosen to bless me.


When the word is in turmoil,
And I long for peace,
I seek Your grace and wisdom,
Knowing You'll see me through.


My faith propels me to work for You,
To move the kingdom forward.
My love produces labor,
And I long to be in service for thee.


Lord, You've promised me peace,
Regardless of what I face.
I know that regardless of the adversity,
Your grace will see me through.

*(Thessalonians 1)*

# Grieve Not For Me

Grieve not for me,
When I am gone.
'Cause we will meet again,
Around the throne of God.


My body lies here,
But my soul has risen,
To be with the King of Kings,
In the comfort and splendor of heaven.


In a twinkling of an eye,
You too will be called,
To join our Savior and Lord,
If you've invited Him to be Lord of your life.


Grieve not for me,
But rejoice instead.
My soul is alive,
Although this body is dead.

*(1 Thessalonians 4: 13 – 18)*

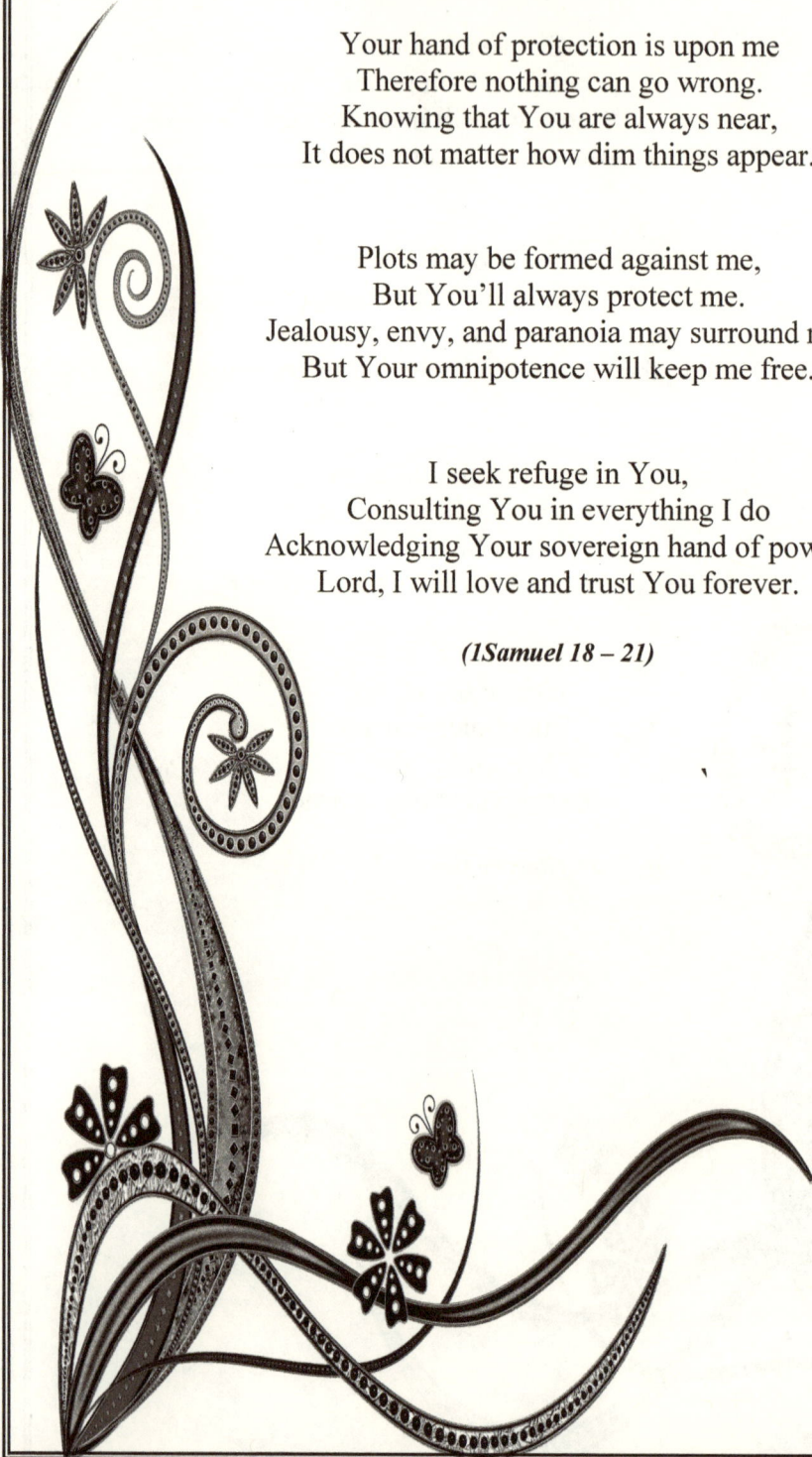

# Hand of Protection

Your hand of protection is upon me
Therefore nothing can go wrong.
Knowing that You are always near,
It does not matter how dim things appear.


Plots may be formed against me,
But You'll always protect me.
Jealousy, envy, and paranoia may surround me,
But Your omnipotence will keep me free.


I seek refuge in You,
Consulting You in everything I do
Acknowledging Your sovereign hand of power,
Lord, I will love and trust You forever.

*(1Samuel 18 – 21)*

## Inspired by Godly Wisdom

I am a child of Almighty God.
Set apart to be Holy unto him.
I am different from others in this world,
Because the glory of God I now behold.

The path I choose to take,
Leads me to the word of God,
I listen to the voice of reason,
But know on God I'll always depend.

Charging hard after things I perceive are best,
Is a thing of the past.
Because in God's will I now rest,
I am careful in my desires,
And look to my God to be inspired.

## Integrity is a Legacy

Integrity is in short supply,
It's a fact we cannot deny.
Greed threatens our character,
But with God we'll be an overcomer.

Integrity is a rare commodity,
In today's self-driven society.
Selfishness threatens our lives,
But with God, we will survive.

Integrity is a legacy,
We can choose to pass on.
Temptations will come our way,
But to God we have only to pray.

# Jesus, Prince of Peace

Jesus, Resurrection and Life,
Thank you for restoring me.
Thank You for pulling me out of hell,
So your mercy and grace, I live to tell.

Jesus, Lord of my soul,
Unto You all praises I bestow,
I honor You with every facet of my being
Body, soul and spirit, I give you everything.

Jesus of Nazareth,
You've proven Yourself to me.
When I thought all hope was lost,
You reached out in love and set me free.

Jesus, Wonderful Counselor,
You are peace for my soul.
Amidst suffering, sadness and strife,
You've calm the raging seas of my life.

# Knowledge of Who I Am

Lord, I know that when others look at me,
Oftentimes I am quickly dismissed.
I admit Lord, that at times when I look at me,
I see what statistics have missed.

Yet I know, Lord,
When You look at me,
You see a life filled with possibilities.
You see an individual created in Your image,
Wrapped in Your love.

I know, in You, I can find the true me.
In my humanity I know I am not much,
So Father, all that I am,
All that I hope to be,
I humbly offer it all to You.

# Living for You

Lord in my humanity,
I'm tempted when my enemies fail,
To rejoice at their demise
Though I know it is wrong.
Lord I struggle to morn,
My enemies' heartaches,
'Cause I dwell on their actions towards me,
And how they've done me wrong.

Lord touch my heart.
Let me take strength from you.
May I forgive my enemies,
'Cause that is what You would do.

Let Your agenda be my desire.
Let Your will be done.
Let my carnal mind decrease,
So that Your plan can create peace.
Let me live Your ordained plan,
And show love to those who wish me wrong.
Let me extend Your love on earth,
Let me be a testimony of mercy and grace.

# Magnifying Jesus

From the depth of my soul,
I glorify You Jesus.
I exalt You Lord,
I magnify You.
I lift You up.

From the depth of my heart,
I acknowledge Your mercy,
Your forgiving power,
Your saving grace,
And your endless mercy.

From the depth of my soul,
I live for You Jesus,
To praise You,
To honor You
To love and serve you.

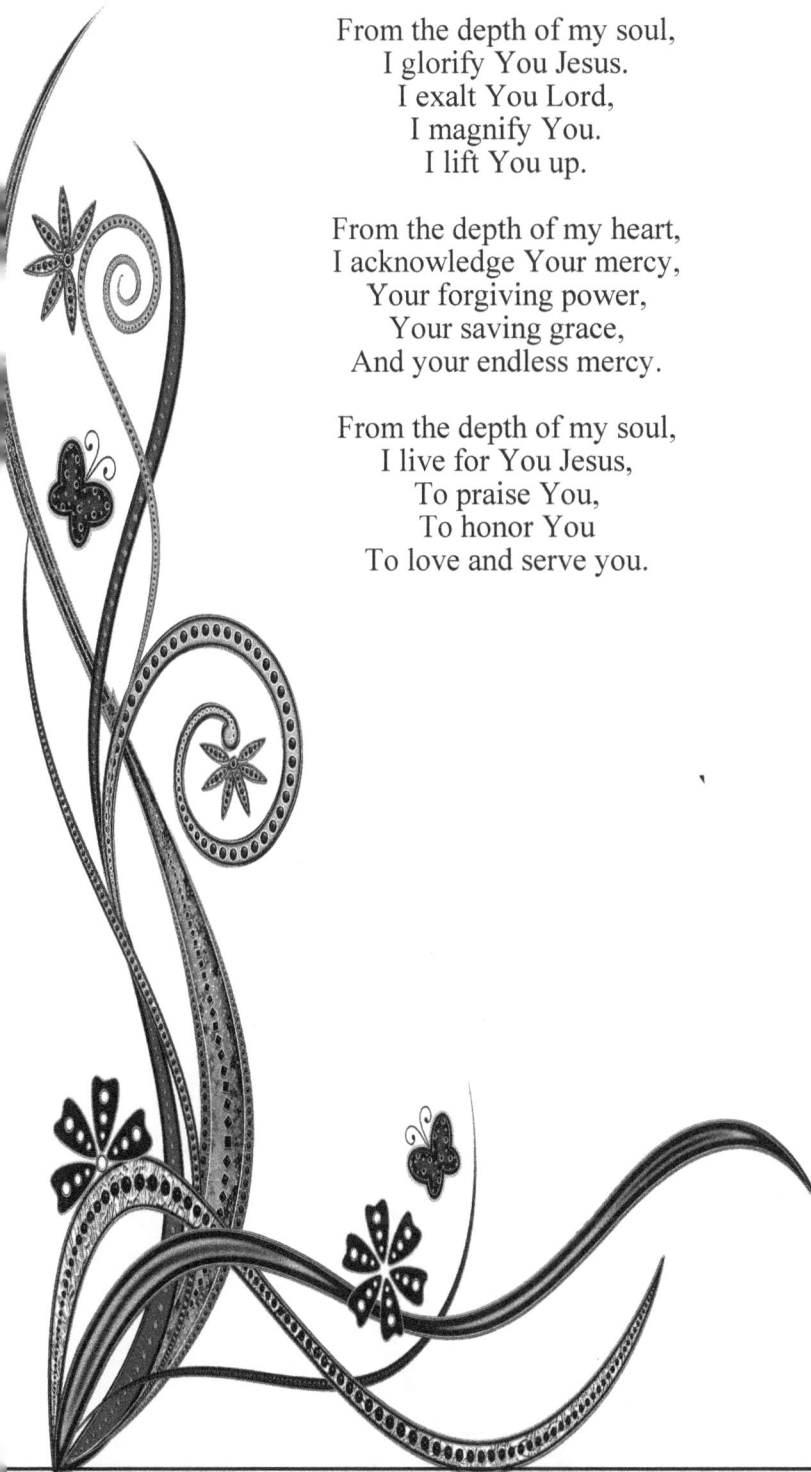

# My Actions Weigh Me Down

Lord, I have done evil in Your sight,
And I walk constantly with the guilt and shame.
It wears me down, and robs my joy.
The weight of my actions is upon me,
It seems too much for me to bear.

I have compounded my agony,
With trying to hide, yet without success,
My moments of weakness.
The pain that burns in my heart,
Seems too much for me to bear.

Lord, I confess my sins to You,
Forgive me this day I pray.
Deliver me from the errors of my ways
So I may honor, praise, and worship You.

*(11 Samuels 12; Ps. 51)*

# Not Shaken

I will not be shaken
In my quest to praise my God,
But rather listen to His Spirit
And rely on His plan.


I will go where He sends me,
And share what is true.
I will minister to souls for God,
So the Savior, people will know.


I will remain focus,
And set my eyes on Christ,
I will remain steadfast,
And trust God with all my heart.


I will be bold in action,
But couples it with consideration.
I will be a witness,
Of God's grace and kindness.

*(Thessalonians 2)*

# Ouch!

Lord, I am guilty.
Guilty of not spending time with You.
Lord, I am guilty.
Guilty of not using my talents and energy for You.


Lord, I am guilty.
Guilty of not glorifying and praising You.
Lord, I am guilty.
Guilty of not seeking and trusting You.


Lord I am guilty.
Guilty of not listening and obeying You.
Lord, I am guilty.
Guilty of being guilty of not dedicating myself to You.

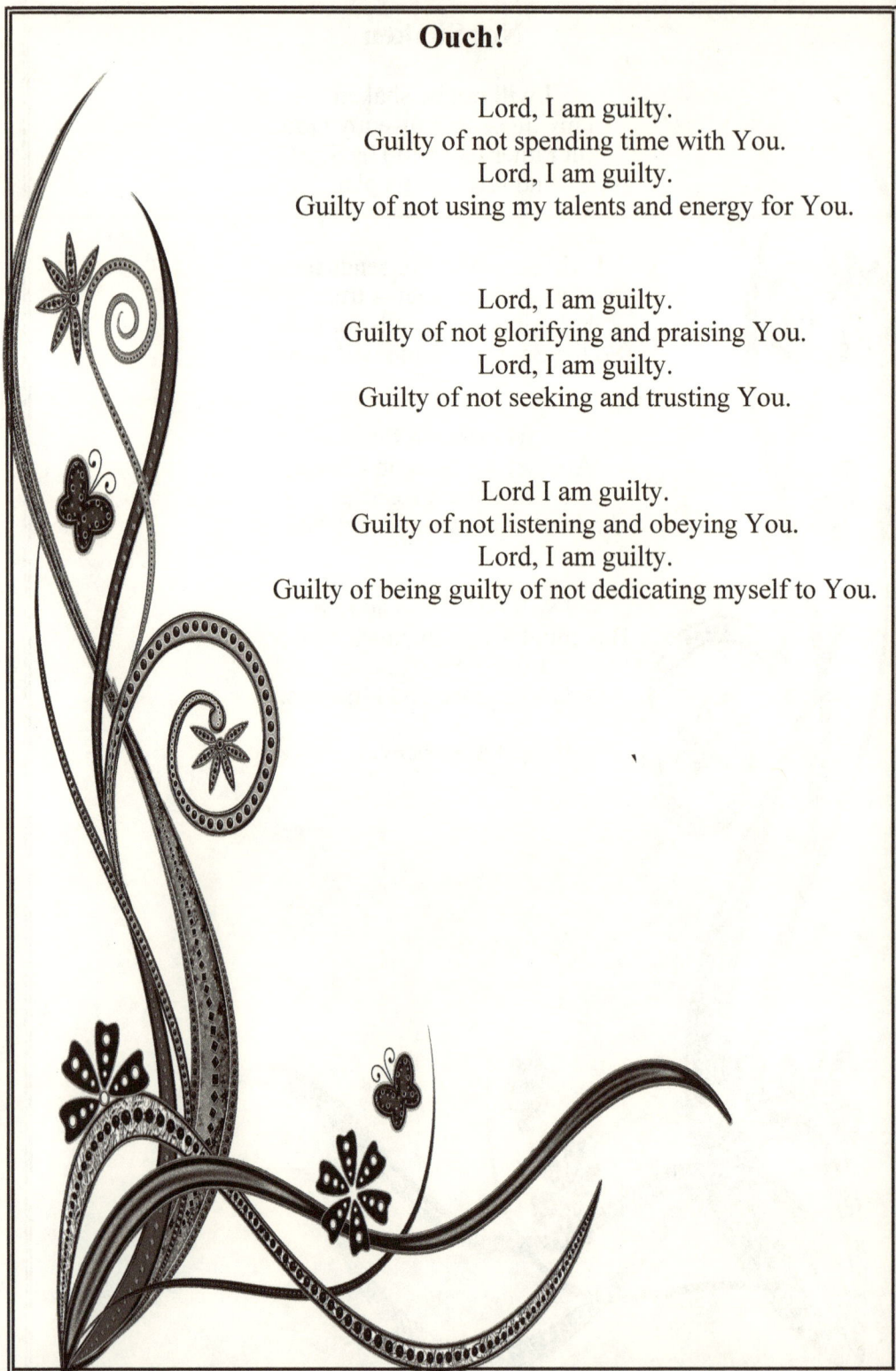

# Perfect Peace

How can You love me, when I've disgraced Your holy name?
Can you still care for me, when I've done so many wrongs?
My heart is aching.  I long to feel Your touch.
Where is that perfect peace?


My heart is burdened, with issues from my past.
My soul gets weary, sometimes I feel completely lost.
I yearn to call for You, but guilt stops me in my path,
And so I ask these questions.


I lay awake at nights, knowing I've done myself wrong.
Oh Lord I could not see, as I drifted from Your plan.
Now I want you to reignite, The Fire in my soul,
But these questions linger still.


There's a raging battle, inside me every day.
I want to do Your will, but my heart is overwhelmed.
Principalities and powers at work, creating doubts in my mind,
So I ask these questions.

Teach me to walk in faith, to reach for Your outstretched hand,
Help me to call on You, and receive my victory.
Remind me that the Holy One, is still in control,
Despite these questions.


Lord I know You love me, though I've disgraced Your Holy name.
Lord You care for me, despite the wrongs that I've done.
My heart is mending, I now can feel Your touch.
You are my perfect peace.
You are my perfect peace.

89

# Pursuit of a Father

So many are hurting,
Crippled with a broken heart.
So many are yearning, for a father we cannot find.


Created in the image of God,
Yet far removed from His character.
Many are longing Lord, for a father we cannot find.
The sense of guilt inherited from Adam
Lingers and multiplies as time unfolds
Affecting everyone!
Many are searching, for a father we cannot find.


Double portion of dysfunction,
Coupled with constant destruction
Plague the heart constantly!
Many are waiting, for a father we cannot find.


Reveal Yourself to us Lord,
As the Father to the fatherless,
Put our yearnings, longings, searching and waiting to rest
Cause You are  Our Father , the Father we can always find.

# Take the Test!

Sometimes it is hard, to step out in faith.
To offer to God, that which we should not withhold.
So… Go ahead and take the test!
Take the test
And you will see,
God will bless you profusely.


His word declares, what we should do,
To help support his kingdom, for his ministry to grow,
So… Go ahead and take the test!
Take the test
And you will see,
God will bless you profusely.


When you give God his tithes and offering
He'll bless you
More than you can possibly imagine,
So… Go ahead and take the test!
Take the test
And you will see,
God will bless you profusely.

# Truth

Many spend their lives searching…
Searching for The Truth,
Not knowing that truth's revealed,
Through Jesus Christ, the Lord!


What is the truth?  What is the truth?
It is just what it is!
What is the truth?
What is the truth?
The Truth is the Word of God.


If you are still longing …
Longing to know The Truth,
Ask Jesus to reveal Himself,
And Truth you'll experience.


What is the truth? Jesus is The Truth!
He's the Son of Almighty God!
What is the truth?
The Truth set you free,
The Truth is Jesus Christ the Lord.

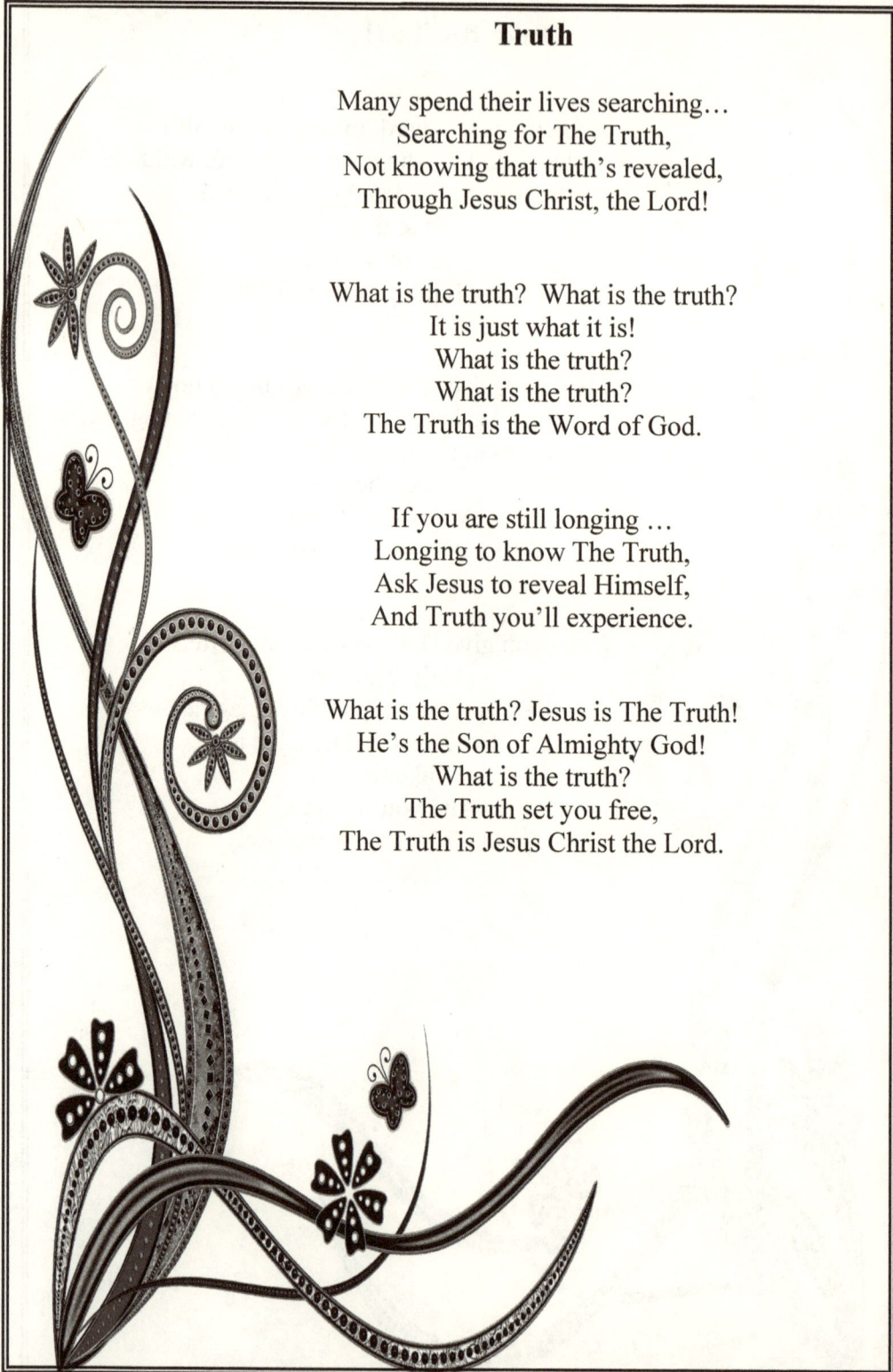

# Voice of God

Listen to the voice of God.
He will direct you.

Listen to the voice of God,
He will guide you.

Listen to the voice of God,
He will protect you.

Listen to the voice of God,
He will reward you.

# Wait on the Lord

The enemy's attack can be ruthless,
Relentlessly he'll pursue you.
Once he gets a foothold in your life,
He will be convinced he has permission to reside.

Resist the devil and he will flee
Listen to the word of God.
Raise your voice and called unto God,
He is God! He will deliver you.

Act not out of fear of what the liar says,
Fearful decisions are hastily made.
Wait on the Lord,
He'll renew your strength,
To withstand the temptations being hurled from hell.

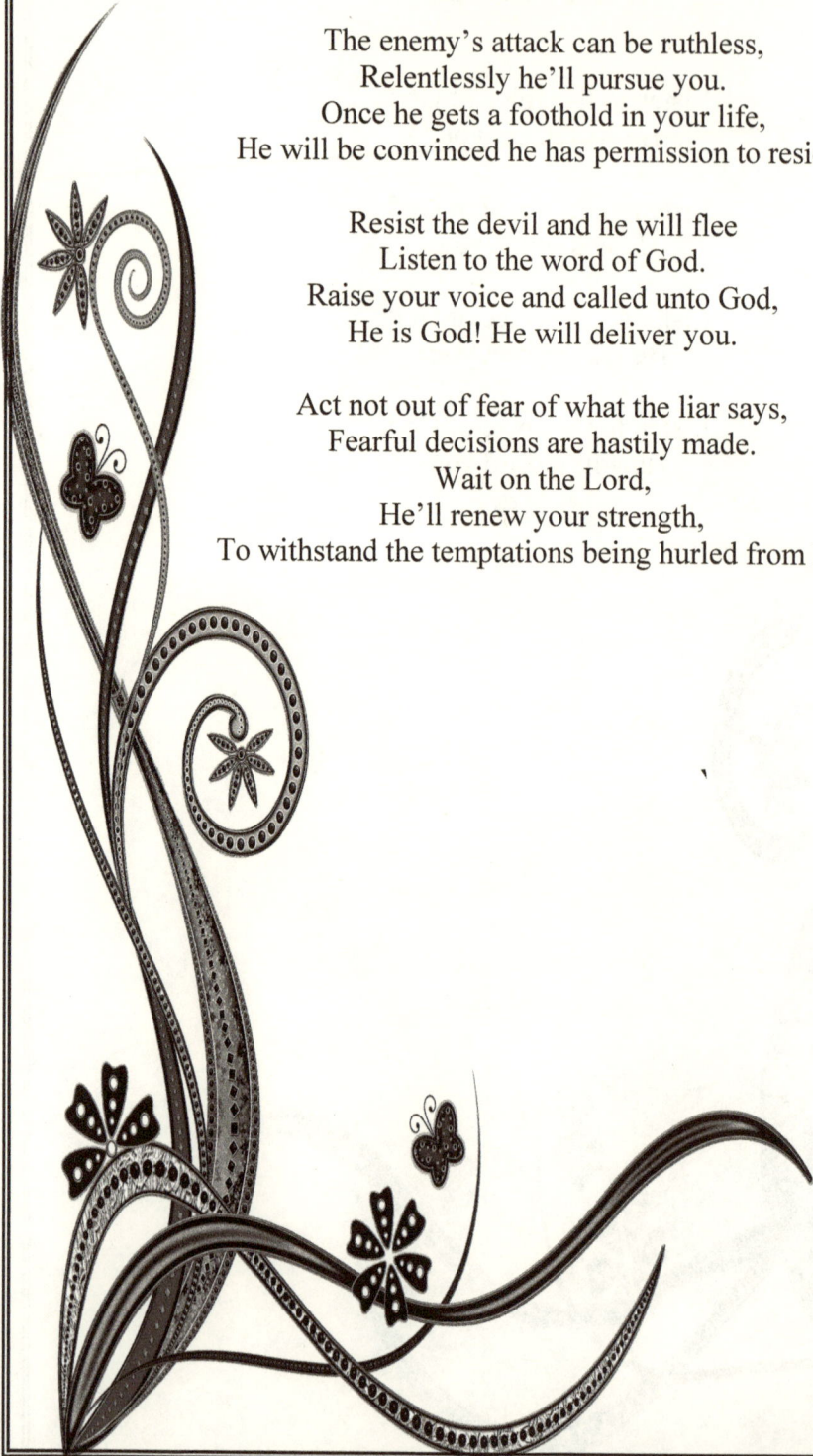

# Your Holy Presence

Lord, I can feel Your Holy Presence,
Surrounding me, hugging me,
Holding me tight,
I can feel Your Holy Presence.


Lord, I can feel Your Holy Presence,
Comforting me, guiding me,
Filling me with joy,
I can feel Your Holy Presence.


Lord, I can feel Your Holy Presence,
Teaching me, correcting me,
Making me strong,
I can feel Your Holy Presence.


Lord, I can feel Your Holy Presence,
Loving me, blessing me,
Giving me life,
I can feel Your Holy Presence.


Lord, I can feel Your Holy Presence,
Forgiving me, changing me,
Making me whole,
I can feel Your Holy Presence.

# You My Lord, Will Remain

You are the one that I serve.
You are the one I adore.
Temptations will come,
And temptations will pass,
But You My Lord, will remain.


You are the one that I praise.
You are the one I embrace.
Friends will come,
And friends will go,
But You My Lord, will remain.


You are the joy in my life.
You are the song that I sing.
Problems will come,
And problems will pass,
But You My Lord, will remain.


You are the King of my life.
You are my heart's desire.
My journey began,
And my journey will end,
But You My Lord, will remain.

www.ingramcontent.com/pod-product-compliance
Lightning Source LLC
LaVergne TN
LVHW011408080426
835511LV00005B/443